Little Boy, Where's Your Joy?

Written by
La'Kesha Walker

MERCY B. CARRUTHERS

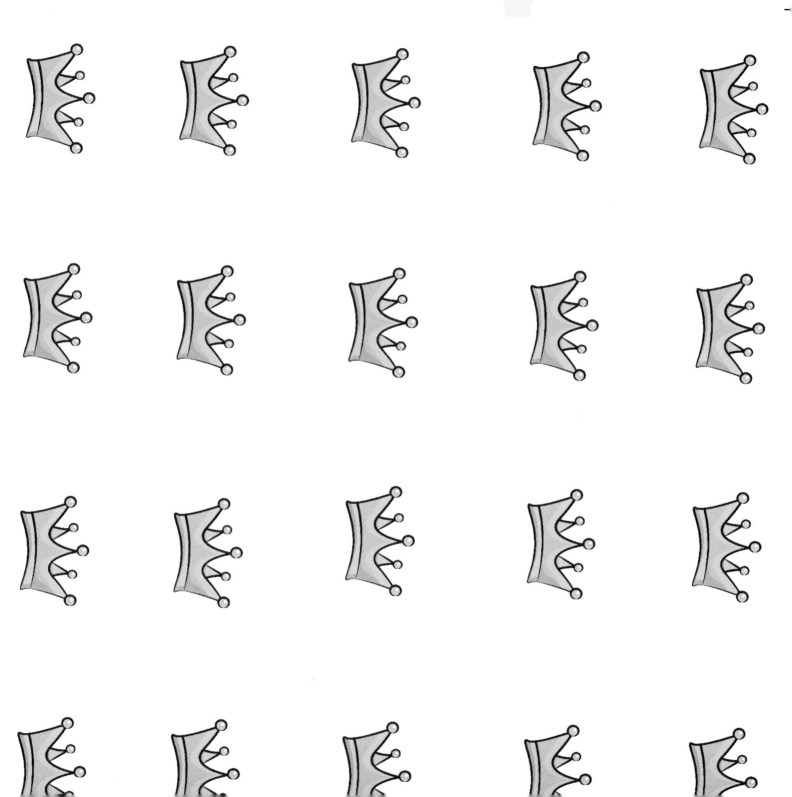

Dedication

Jason and Ahmir, through every cloudy day and every dark night, my biggest prayer for you is that you be the brightest light. May you never lose your joy.

There once was a boy named Jason, his skin was a beautiful brown,

But for some strange reason, that made the boy feel down.

He didn't understand why his nose was spread wide,

Or why his full lips made him feel sad inside.

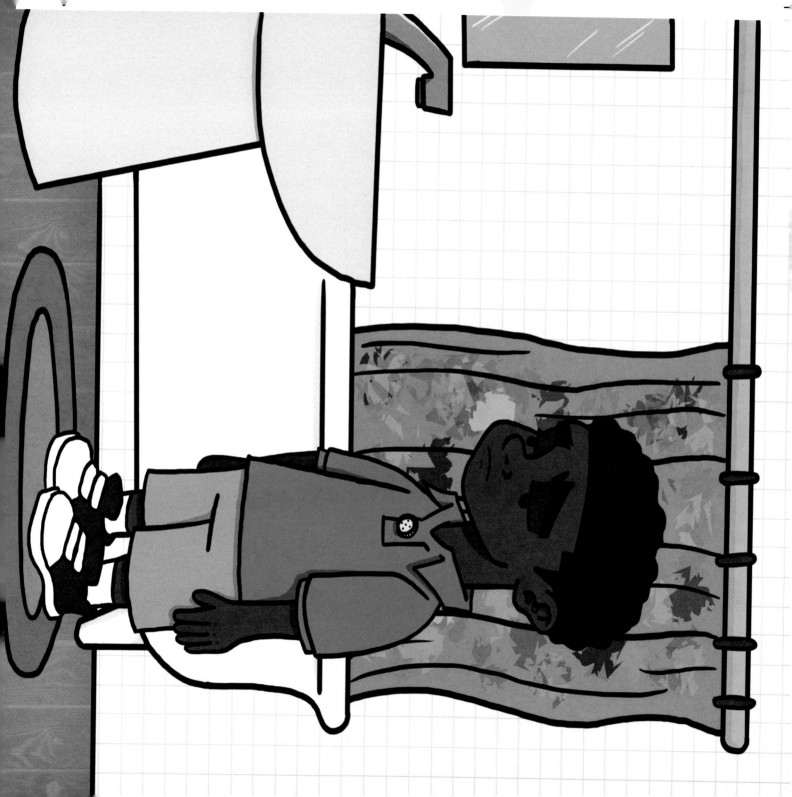

That night at dinner, Jason played with his food,
To no surprise, his mommy noticed his mood.
"Jason, my baby, why the long face? Your food
will get cold if you don't pick up the pace."
Little Jason took a bite, slowly chewed and said,
"Mommy, there's one thing I can't get out of my
head."

Putting down her fork, his mom could see this
was serious.

"Tell mommy what's wrong, now you've got me curious."

"I just feel sad that I don't look like all of my friends."

"But that's not a bad thing." His mom said with a grin.

"You look the way you do because you have such strong genes,

All of your ancestors were kings and queens."

"Just look at those hands, imagine what they could do one day,

Like James Smith, the first black doctor in the USA.

He used his hands to treat the ill and the hurt,
He gave medicine when needed; he did great work."

"He sounds very important." Jason said as he looked at his hands.

"You're important too, baby, that's what I hope you understand."

"What else mommy? Tell me more about me." Jason began to perk up, his face filling with glee.

"Alright, I will, but eat your food, little boy." His mother said, smiling with joy.

As Jason ate, his mother took him all in,
Trying to decide where to begin.
"Hurry up, mommy, I'm eating, are you looking?!"
"Alright, baby, let me tell you about cooking.
Rufus Estes was a great black cook,
He used his nose to create recipes for a book.
One of the very first chefs in all of black history,
At first he kept all of his dishes a mystery.
He smelled all of his cooking with a nose like yours,
He cooked for the president and went on book tours.

Many, many people bought his book for their homes,

Over time, his recipes became like their own.
He paved the way for black chefs down the line,
Even your grandma uses his recipes sometimes."
"That's awesome, mommy, I never would have guessed".

"So you see, my baby boy, with that nose, you are blessed."

"What about my ears? There's nothing special about those."

"Jason, you are special from your head to your toes."

"Do you know there was a man who used his ears to listen to the people?

He fought against segregation and made the schools equal."

"You see, there was a time when kids went to school apart,

The blacks and the whites couldn't sit together to learn art."

"Or reading and writing amongst other things,
But Dr. Kenneth Bancroft was amongst the black kings."

"You can sit next to Susie and Amir and learn math,
Because he believed that every student deserved the same path."

"I'm done with my food, mom, can I have some pie?"
"Okay, baby boy, want to hear about your eyes?"
"Of course I do, mommy! But don't I just use them to look?"

"You do, my boy, like I do when I cook."

"Guess who used their eyes to do good?
His name was Frederick Douglass and he fought
for womanhood."

"He saw a vision of women having voting rights,
And that was only one of his victorious fights."
"He saw a world without slavery and helped it to
end,

Despite all his troubles, he refused to bend."
"So, your eyes, little boy, can see whatever you
want to see,

You could make history like he did, don't you
agree?"

"I do now, mommy, and this pie is so yummy!"
Jason exclaimed, while rubbing his tummy.
"I'm glad you're enjoying it, but don't talk while
you chew.

Oh, that reminds me, I've got one more for you."

"There lived another man who knew we could be great,

So he spoke up to the people who only showed hate."

"He used his mouth to voice his thoughts on the way we were treated,

He helped create a great organization, which we desperately needed."

"The National Association for the Advancement of Colored People

Made it possible for us all to feel equal."

W.E.B. Du Bois was a very smart man, and if he can speak up,

Then Jason, you can."

It's important for you to know and love all the things,
That can help you make history, just like these kings.

Made in the USA
Coppell, TX
05 June 2020